Mythical Creatures

UNICORNS

by Theresa Jarosz Alberti

www.focusreaders.com

Focus Readers is distributed by North Star Editions:
sales@northstareditions.com | 888-417-0195

Produced for Focus Readers by Red Line Editorial.

Photographs ©: CoreyFord/iStockphoto, cover, 1, 7; Pobytov/iStockphoto, 4–5, 14–15; RFStock/iStockphoto, 8–9, 29; unUnlucky/Shutterstock Images, 11; travelview/Shutterstock Images, 13; Monoceros/The Rochester Bestiary/British Library, 16; Christopher PB/Shutterstock Images, 18; Flip Nicklin/Minden Pictures/Newscom, 20–21; Fratelli Alinari IDEA S.p.A./Corbis Historical/Getty Images, 22–23; mscornelius/iStockphoto, 24; Everett - Art/Shutterstock Images, 26

ISBN
978-1-63517-904-0 (hardcover)
978-1-64185-006-3 (paperback)
978-1-64185-208-1 (ebook pdf)
978-1-64185-107-7 (hosted ebook)

Library of Congress Control Number: 2018931704

Printed in the United States of America
Mankato, MN
May, 2018

About the Author

Theresa Jarosz Alberti called herself a writer when she was 10 years old. She wrote many stories and poems. Now she enjoys writing for both kids and adults. She lives in Minneapolis, Minnesota.

TABLE OF CONTENTS

CHAPTER 1

A UNICORN'S DAY

A unicorn rests deep in the forest. He wakes up to a sunny day. He drinks from a flowing stream. A soft breeze blows his mane. Around him, birds tweet. Flowers grow in the sun.

 A unicorn relaxes in a peaceful field.

The unicorn's ears flicker. Horse hooves pound against the ground. Voices call out. The hunters have returned. They want to capture the mysterious unicorn. Nobody has ever caught a unicorn. But the hunters are determined. They will not give up.

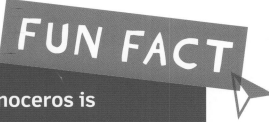

FUN FACT

The **constellation** Monoceros is shaped like a unicorn. It includes 146 visible stars.

 A unicorn family hides from hunters.

The unicorn gallops through the trees. He knows the forest well. He hides in a cave until the hunters ride away. Then, the unicorn comes out. He stays very quiet in case the hunters return.

CHAPTER 2

UNICORNS IN HISTORY

Long ago, people reported seeing unicorns. In Latin, *uni* means "one" and *cornu* means "horn." Put together, *unicorn* describes an animal with one horn. Soon, people began telling stories of unicorns.

The gates of Buckingham Palace in London, England, feature a unicorn statue.

Unicorn **myths** come from all over the world. Unicorns were first mentioned in writing around 2700 BCE. These stories came from Asia. In the 300s BCE, a Greek historian wrote about unicorns. His name was Ctesias. He had heard of the creature from Indian travelers.

FUN FACT

In the 1200s CE, explorer Marco Polo claimed to see a unicorn. He described it as an ugly beast.

 The Indian rhinoceros lives in northern India and Nepal.

The travelers claimed they had seen unicorns. However, they most likely saw a rhinoceros. The Indian rhinoceros has only one horn.

Unicorns **fascinate** humans. In the **Middle Ages**, an artist created the Unicorn Tapestries. The tapestries, or wall hangings, tell a story. Pictures on the cloth show men hunting a unicorn. In the same period, authors wrote books about mythical creatures. These

FUN FACT

In the 1400s CE, people in Scotland used coins with images of unicorns on them.

 Today, the Unicorn Tapestries hang in an art museum in New York.

books were called bestiaries. Many bestiaries included descriptions of unicorns. Writers described how unicorns looked and behaved. They thought the creatures had magical powers.

13

CHAPTER 3

UNICORNS AROUND THE WORLD

In many early stories, the unicorn has a body of a goat. On its head is a short, colorful horn. In other stories, the unicorn looks like a horse. This type of unicorn has a long, white horn.

The image of the white, horse-like unicorn is most popular today.

 This brown unicorn is featured in a bestiary from the 1200s CE.

Ctesias described unicorns in his writings. He said that unicorns are large and white. The unicorn's horn is red, black, and white. The animal also has a purple head and blue eyes.

But not all unicorns are white. In stories, they can also be black, brown, or golden. Many unicorns have traits of other animals. They may have a lion's tail or goat's beard.

Some countries have their own unicorn myths. For example, the Chinese unicorn is called a kylin.

FUN FACT

In Vietnam, people celebrate the Mid-Autumn Festival. Dancers in unicorn costumes perform in a parade.

 Unlike the white unicorn, the kylin often has many colors.

The kylin has a body of a deer and the head of a dragon. It is covered in fish-like scales. Other Asian countries have similar unicorns.

Persian **legends** tell of the karkadann. This creature looks like a buffalo. But each of its feet has three hooves. It also has a horn of gold.

A unicorn horn is called an alicorn. This term also refers to a unicorn with wings.

FUN FACT

Alicorns appear in the show *My Little Pony.* The alicorn ponies are princesses.

UNICORNS TODAY

Narwhals are called the unicorns of the sea. But the narwhal is not a myth. It is a type of whale. Narwhals live in Arctic waters. Similar to unicorns, they have one horn. But the narwhal's horn is actually a tooth. It has a spiral pattern. The tooth can reach up to 10 feet (3.0 m) in length.

Long ago, people valued unicorn horns. However, the horns were fake. In the 1500s, England's Queen Elizabeth I owned a unicorn horn. It was actually a narwhal tooth. The tooth cost as much as a castle.

The narwhal's tooth is made of ivory.

CHAPTER 4

THE MYSTERY OF THE UNICORN

According to legend, unicorns live in forests. They feed on grass and moss. Most unicorns live in quiet solitude. Humans rarely see them. However, some unicorns are drawn to beautiful **maidens**.

In some myths, maidens are able to calm wild unicorns.

 A unicorn chews on grass by a quiet pond.

In most myths, unicorns are gentle creatures. They are wise and **compassionate**. Asian unicorns are kind to all living things. They walk very softly. They do not want

24

to hurt insects or blades of grass.
These unicorns are signs of power
and peace.

Other unicorns are not peaceful.
The karkadann is a fierce warrior. It
fights animals such as elephants.
The karkadann can even change the
shape of its body.

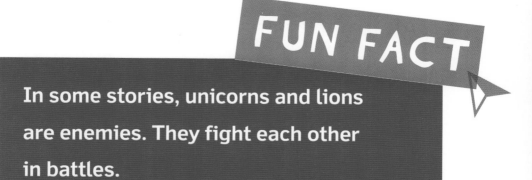

FUN FACT

In some stories, unicorns and lions
are enemies. They fight each other
in battles.

 Hunters surround a resting unicorn.

All unicorns have magical powers.
A unicorn horn can **counteract**
poison. The unicorn touches its
horn to water. This makes the water

safe to drink. Unicorns use their power to help animals and humans.

In stories, people hunt unicorns. But unicorns are hard to catch. The hunters use maidens to **lure** the unicorn. Then, they kill the unicorn. They make medicine from its horn. In the Middle Ages, people thought unicorn horns could cure illness.

Today, few people believe in unicorns. But stories of unicorns remain popular. These stories keep the mystery of the unicorn alive.

FOCUS ON
UNICORNS

Write your answers on a separate piece of paper.

1. Write a sentence summarizing one of the unicorns described in Chapter 3.

2. How are unicorns different from other mythical creatures? How are they similar?

3. Long ago, which animal did people think was a unicorn?

    A. lion

    B. rhinoceros

    C. elephant

4. Why are unicorns hard to catch?

    A. They injure and kill humans.

    B. They play tricks on humans.

    C. They hide from humans.

5. What does **determined** mean in this book?

*Nobody has ever caught a unicorn. But the hunters are **determined**. They will not give up.*

    A. afraid of wild animals

    B. fixed on reaching a goal

    C. too tired to continue

6. What does **solitude** mean in this book?

*Most unicorns live in quiet **solitude**. Humans rarely see them.*

    A. a place away from others

    B. a fantasy land

    C. a busy, crowded area

Answer key on page 32.

GLOSSARY

compassionate
Showing care and concern for others.

constellation
A group of stars that form a pattern or picture in the sky.

counteract
To act against something.

fascinate
To draw attention or interest.

legends
Well-known stories from the past that are often untrue.

lure
To convince someone to come near.

maidens
Young, unmarried women.

Middle Ages
A period in European history that lasted from the 400s CE to the 1400s CE.

myths
Well-known, fictional stories common to a group of people.

TO LEARN MORE

BOOKS

Atwood, Megan. *Unicorns*. Minneapolis: Abdo
Publishing, 2014.

Peabody, Erin. *Unicorns*. New York: Little Bee
Books, 2018.

Sautter, A. J. *A Field Guide to Griffins, Unicorns,
and Other Mythical Beasts*. Mankato, MN:
Capstone Press, 2015.

NOTE TO EDUCATORS

Visit **www.focusreaders.com** to find lesson plans,
activities, links, and other resources related to
this title.

INDEX

Answer Key: **1.** Answers will vary; **2.** Answers will vary; **3.** B; **4.** C; **5.** B; **6.** A